Come to My Tea Party

Kindness and Friendship for Young Ladies

Text and Paintings by

SANDY LYNAM CLOUGH

HARVEST HOUSE™ PUBLISHERS

EUGENE, OREGON

To Sarah
Elizabeth
Clough

who, like all children,
brought joy at her birth

Come to My
Tea Party

Copyright © 2002 by Sandy Lynam Clough
Published by Harvest House Publishers
Eugene, Oregon 97402
www.harvesthousepublishers.com

Library of Congress Cataloging-in-Publication Data
Clough, Sandy Lynam, 1948-
  Come to my tea party / Sandy Lynam Clough.
    p. cm.
Summary: On her birthday, Colleen receives a tea set and toys representing faith, hope, and love, then organizes six tea parties to share those gifts with others and to seek the final one, joy. Includes recipes.
ISBN-13: 978-0-7369-0670-8
ISBN-10: 0-7369-0670-3 (alk. paper)
[1. Afternoon teas—Fiction. 2. Parties—Fiction. 3. Friendship—Fiction. 4. Conduct of life—Fiction.] I. Title.
PZ7.C62395 Co 2002
[Fic]—dc21

2002001525

All works of art reproduced in this book are copyrighted by Sandy Lynam Clough and may not be reproduced without the artist's permission. For information regarding art prints featured in this book, please contact:

    Sandy Clough Studios
    P.O. Box 85
    Powder Springs, GA 30127-0085
    (800) 447-8409
    www.sandyclough.com
    www.sandysteasociety.com

Design and production by Koechel Peterson & Associates, Minneapolis, Minnesota

Scripture quotations are taken from *The Holy Bible, New Century Version*, Copyright © 1987, 1988, 1991 by Word Publishing, Nashville, TN 37214. Used by permission.

All rights reserved. No part of this publication may be reproduced, stored in a retrieval system, or transmitted in any form or by any means—electronic, mechanical, digital, photocopy, recording, or any other—except for brief quotations in printed reviews, without the prior permission of the publisher.

Printed in Hong Kong

07 08 09 10 11 / N G / 10 9 8 7 6 5 4 3

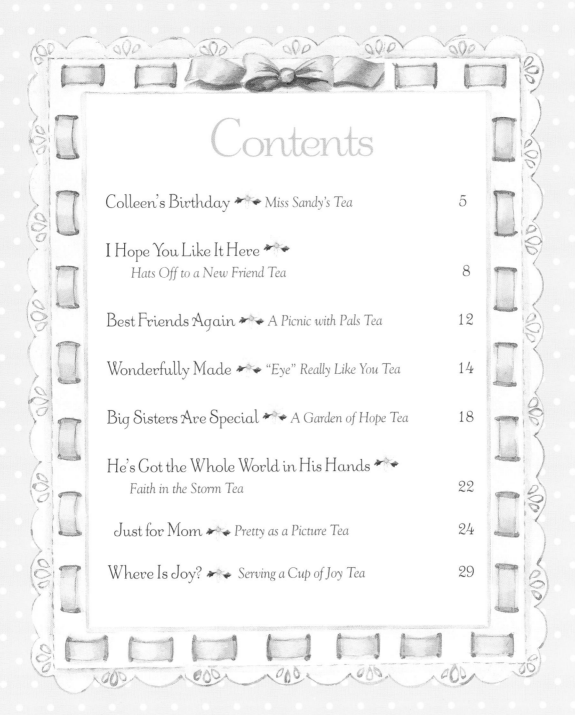

Contents

Colleen's
Birthday
Miss Sandy's Tea

Colleen walked along the path to Miss Sandy's Tearoom with her mother, Suzette. A blue butterfly caught her eye, and she chased it as far as the picket fence. Then she skipped to catch up with her mother. Running in her dress-up dress would never do!

Suzette stopped at the gate to Miss Sandy's Tearoom. "Colleen," said her mother with a smile, "you and I have had many tea parties together, but today your birthday surprise is a tea party with Miss Sandy."

"You mean all by myself, like a grown-up lady?" asked Colleen.

"Yes!" laughed her mother. "Miss Sandy is at the door now." And she blew Colleen a kiss as she watched her try not to run down the sidewalk to the tearoom. As Colleen reached the porch, she turned and waved goodbye to her mother as Miss Sandy invited her in.

"Happy Birthday, Colleen!" Miss Sandy greeted her warmly as she took her by the hand and led her to a beautifully decorated table with ribbon streamers and balloons. A ring of daisies surrounded a cake with pink dots of icing. "You can sit here, at the seat of honor, today."

"Thank you, Miss Sandy," said Colleen as she gently sat down, practicing her very best manners. Looking around the table, Colleen couldn't help but notice three other chairs— in one was a teddy bear, in one was a bunny, and in one was a doll.

"I want to introduce you to some new friends," said Miss Sandy.

Colleen's eyes opened wide as the bunny said, "I hope your birthday's the happiest ever!"

Then the teddy bear said, "I know it will be the happiest ever!"

And the doll added, "I just love birthdays!"

Colleen was speechless!

"Colleen," said Miss Sandy, "meet your three new friends—Rosebeary, Bunnita, and Upsi-Daisy. They are gifts for you—and you can take them home after our tea party!"

Mother was right, Colleen thought, *this is a birthday surprise!*

As Miss Sandy poured raspberry tea, she said, "You already know that tea parties bring friends together. We talk about 'taking tea' together, but tea parties are more about giving than taking. We can offer our friends more than delicious treats and a warm cup of tea."

"What else can you offer at a tea party?" asked Colleen.

"You can offer faith, hope, and love to your friends," suggested Miss Sandy.

Colleen was about to ask "how?" when Miss Sandy handed her a beautiful pink-and-white striped hatbox with a yellow-and-white polka-dot lid. There was a daisy tied in the bow on top. "May I open it?" she asked.

"Oh, yes, please!" said Miss Sandy. "This is my birthday gift for you!"

"But I already have the gift of my new friends."

"You'll see," Miss Sandy smiled.

Colleen opened the hatbox and squealed in delight, "My own tea set!"

Nestled in the hatbox was a beautiful yellow-and-white polka-dot tea set trimmed with lace and daisies. On the lid of the teapot was written, "Serve each other with love." On the lid of the sugar bowl was written, "Be sweet to each other," and on the cookie plate was written, "The very best thing is love." Each of the teacups had one word inscribed inside: one said "Faith," one said "Hope," one said "Love," and one said "Joy."

"Thank you! Thank you!" said Colleen. "I can share faith, hope, and love with my friends by using this tea set."

"Yes," said Miss Sandy, "but there is a little more to it than that. Faith, hope, and love have to be shared from your heart. Can you think of tea parties that will show faith, hope, or love to your friends?"

"I can try," volunteered Colleen.

"We can help!" chimed Rosebeary, Bunnita, and Upsi-Daisy.

"Rosebeary will help you share faith, Bunnita will help you share hope, and Upsi-Daisy will help you share love. In fact, Upsi-Daisy is almost like a thermometer of love and kindness."

"A thermometer?" giggled Colleen.

"Yes," said Miss Sandy. "She is so tender-hearted that it just turns her whole world upside down to see someone be unkind, and it makes her blue. That's why we call her Upsi-Daisy. But, when someone rights a wrong, she is right-side up and sunny again!"

"I can't wait to begin!" Colleen exclaimed. "But wait, what about the 'joy' cup? Who will teach me about joy?"

"That birthday surprise will have to wait. I want you to come back for another tea party and tell me about the tea parties you have had with your friends."

"Thank you, Miss Sandy. This is the best birthday ever! And the fun is just beginning!" cheered Colleen.

These three things continue forever: faith, hope, and love. And the greatest of these is love.

1 Corinthians 13:13

I Hope
You Like It Here

Hats Off to a New Friend Tea

"Look at my new tea set," said Colleen to her best friend Maggie. "Who could we invite to our first tea party?"

"My mother says the new neighbors have a girl about our age. Her name is Caroline," answered Maggie.

"She's probably hoping for some friends," suggested Bunnita.

"That's it!" declared Colleen with excitement. "Together we can say 'I Hope You Like It Here' by offering Caroline tea and our friendship!"

"How can we make it special?" Maggie was wondering as she looked at Rosebeary, Bunnita, and Upsi-Daisy. They always looked like they were dressed for tea.

"Hats!" she said. "We can have a dress-up tea and wear hats. Wait a minute," Maggie paused, "what if Caroline doesn't have a hat?"

"We can make hats for all of us before the tea party. I know my mother will help," Colleen assured her.

Colleen was right. Her mother, Suzette, knew just what to do. For each of the three hats she took a paper dinner plate (turned upside down) and glued a paper soup bowl upside down in the center of the bottom side of the plate with a hot glue gun. Then she cut a hole out of the center of the plate underneath the bowl—creating a crown for their heads.

Maggie and Caroline had a fun afternoon decorating the hats with silk flowers, beads,

and ribbons—even tying a length of tulle around one. Colleen's mother supervised with the hot glue gun. Then the girls carefully wrote out an invitation to their tea party and took it to their new neighbor's house.

The next morning at ten o'clock, Caroline knocked timidly on Colleen's front door. The door opened wide.

"Hi, Caroline! I'm Colleen."

"I'm Maggie."

"Welcome to the neighborhood!" they said in unison.

"Oh, thank you, Colleen and Maggie," said Caroline, timidly at first. Then she added with great relief and enthusiasm, "I was hoping for some friends in my new neighborhood."

The three girls had fun looking at each other's dress-up clothes with long beads and boas. Scooting and shuffling around in their mother's high heel shoes, they played like they were grown-up ladies and admired each other's dresses.

Colleen had saved the hats for teatime and carefully placed the hats they had made for

each girl in her chair. She had done a little extra work after Maggie had gone home. There was now a surprise for her too—a little blue bird on her hat!

Maggie began to enjoy her role impersonating a society lady a little too much, becoming very dramatic—and a little silly! "Dahlings," she said, "I am absolutely famished." She swept her hand across her forehead

TEATIME TREAT
Chocolate-Covered Pretzels

Soften white chocolate chips in the microwave (check the chip package for microwave temperatures and time). Next, dip your favorite pretzels into the chocolate. Be careful when you do this because the chocolate is quite warm. Place your delicious creations on waxed paper so they can cool and harden.

and fell into a chair. But it wasn't her chair—it was Colleen's. And she completely smashed Colleen's beautiful teatime hat!

Tears began to well up in Colleen's eyes. She had tried so hard to make this a perfectly nice tea party so that Caroline would like them. Without thinking, she blurted out, "You smashed my hat, Maggie!"

"But, I didn't mean to…" started Maggie.

"You didn't have to be so silly. Now you've ruined my tea party!"

Maggie's feelings were hurt and she fired back, "Who cares about your old tea party!"

Not thinking at all about her guest, Colleen retorted, "Who cares about you! Why don't you go home!"

"Gladly," snapped Maggie. As she turned to go, she tipped over the table. Teacups were tumbling and cookies were crumbling.

Bunnita's ears fell down in front of her face. "I can't bear to watch," she said to Rosebeary. "Tell me when it's over."

"It's not over yet," said Rosebeary. "Upsi-Daisy is upside down and blue!"

Caroline ran home in tears, and Colleen sat down on the floor and cried too.

Colleen's mother peeked into the room. She came in and sat down beside Colleen. "I don't think," she said softly, "that this is exactly what Miss Sandy had in mind."

"I'm sorry," said Colleen, between sniffs. "I wanted so much for it to be nice."

"I know that you feel sorry," said her mother. "But do you know that you were wrong?"

"But Maggie was wrong, too!" protested Colleen.

"You can only choose the right behavior for yourself," reminded her mother. "Besides, she was your guest." She stood up. "Maybe," she said thoughtfully, "you could think about what went wrong here and how to make it right while you clean up this mess."

"Yes, ma'am," Colleen replied.

When Colleen thought for a while about how she had accused her friend of smashing the hat on purpose and had criticized her and called her silly, she was as blue as Upsi-Daisy and felt sorry about her behavior. Upsi-Daisy, Rosebeary, and Bunnita quietly helped her clean up the mess.

"You know, we still haven't done what we set out to do—have a nice tea party to welcome Caroline," ventured Rosebeary.

"And Caroline is still hoping for friends," added Bunnita. "And now Maggie is too."

"Do you think they both would forgive me if I told them I was wrong and that I was sorry?" asked Colleen.

"I have faith!" declared Rosebeary.

"I have hope!" declared Bunnita.

"That would be lovely," sighed Upsi-Daisy.

"Do you think they would come to another tea party?" wondered Colleen.

"There's nothing like a picnic," suggested Rosebeary, "to clear the air." ⋙

Be kind and loving to each other.

Ephesians 4:32

Best Friends Again

A Picnic with Pals Tea

Bunnita and Rosebeary each took one of Upsi-Daisy's hands and helped her up on the soft quilt in Colleen's wagon.

While Colleen was packing up her teacups and teapots, her mother had made some sandwiches and packed some apple cinnamon tea. Bunnita, expecting a celebration, had decorated the wagon with ribbon streamers and daisies. As they settled in, Rosebeary passed out sunglasses. "We're taking this tea party on the road!"

Colleen picked up the handle and started pulling the wagon down the sidewalk toward Maggie's house.

"Look!" Bunnita called out. Coming down the sidewalk toward them was Maggie.

"Hold on to your hat!" laughed Rosebeary.

The wagon lunged forward as Colleen hurried to meet Maggie.

"I'm sorry," they both said at once, almost out of breath.

"I was wrong to be unkind to you," Colleen began.

"And I was wrong to spoil your party," admitted Maggie.

"Unkindness spoils everything," agreed Upsi-Daisy.

"Will you forgive me?" they both asked each other, answering "yes" at the same time.

"Want to have a tea party?" asked Colleen with a smile.

From behind her back Maggie pulled a new hat she had made for Colleen. "And I've got cookies! Let's go get Caroline."

Soon they were at Caroline's door. "Would you forgive us for being unkind to each other and join us for a tea party picnic in the park?" they asked.

"Oh, yes! And I'll pull the wagon!" volunteered Caroline.

As soon as they got to the park, a sunny Upsi-Daisy hopped out of the wagon, right-side up, and spread the quilt for tea.

Together the girls had a delightful tea party. Caroline told them all about the place where she used to live and the pony at her grandmother's farm. After tea, the girls had a fun time making bracelets and necklaces out of clover chains. They found empty acorns that made miniature pretend teacups and big leaves for pretend plates.

"Uh-oh," said Maggie, as she noticed Caroline's mother coming toward them, "it might be time for you to go home."

With a basket behind her back, Caroline's mother walked over to them and leaned forward. "I thought you might like 'favors' for your tea party." She pulled the basket from behind her back and put it down. Suddenly kittens were everywhere, dressed in doll clothes for a tea party!

"Oh, thank you!" the girls giggled. "How can we ever give them up?"

"You don't have to," she smiled, "your mothers said that you can each keep one."

The girls were so excited!

"Tea party days are the very best days!" cheered Maggie.

"And love is the very best thing!" declared Colleen.

"I had faith!" asserted Rosebeary.

"I never gave up hope!" added Bunnita.

"It is lovely!" smiled Upsi-Daisy.

A friend loves you all the time.
Proverbs 17:17

Wonderfully Made

"Eye" Really Like You Tea

As Colleen, Caroline, and Maggie took a stroll down the street with their dolls in their carriages, Colleen thought to herself, "I wonder who needs faith or hope or love today?"

Just then, she saw her friend Amber on her front porch swing. Colleen waved to her, but with a quick wave back, Amber just ran inside.

"Why did she do that?" Colleen was puzzled.

"She has new glasses and won't come out and play," confided Maggie.

"But I would like to meet her," said Caroline.

"You would like her," agreed Maggie and Colleen.

"She needs hope that no one will laugh because she looks different," Bunnita said sympathetically.

"And she needs faith that God did a very good job when he made her and that she is wonderfully made and very special—with or without glasses," Rosebeary added.

"The love of her friends can help her see that," suggested Upsi-Daisy.

"Are you thinking what I'm thinking?" asked Colleen, looking at Maggie and Caroline.

"Yes," said Caroline, "let's have a 'I Really Like *You*' tea party."

"No," said Maggie smiling, "let's make it an '*Eye* Really Like You' tea party!"

The girls had no time for strolling now! With Bunnita, Rosebeary, and Upsi-Daisy hanging on to their hats in the carriages with the dolls, the girls hurried home to plan their tea party.

The girls were stumped in the middle of their planning. They were trying to encourage Amber about wearing glasses without embarrassing her. Caroline finally said with a sigh, "If only everybody wore glasses then Amber wouldn't feel different!"

"That's it!" Colleen's eyes lit up. "We will all wear glasses at the tea party."

"But we don't all have glasses," Caroline said sadly.

"But we can make some out of old sunglasses," suggested Colleen.

"Yes, we can pop out the dark lenses and decorate the frames. Glasses can be fun!" continued Maggie.

Amber couldn't resist an invitation to a tea party just for her. But, even so, when she arrived at Colleen's house the next afternoon, she was so self-conscious that she took off her glasses and slipped them in her pocket before she rang the doorbell. Colleen opened the door and welcomed her friend with a big smile.

Thank you for tea so warm and friends so kind

Then she introduced her to Caroline saying, "Caroline, this is my friend Amber. I know that you're going to like her."

"I already do," replied Caroline sincerely.

They all joined Maggie, who was placing the sandwiches and tea goodies on the table. They sat down, and after Colleen said a prayer of thanks for friends and teatime treats, Amber opened her eyes and began to giggle. "You all have glasses on."

Colleen's glasses had a lace ruffle around each eye and a little dollhouse-sized teacup and saucer on each side. Maggie had silk daisies around her glasses and a little bee glued to one flower. Caroline's glasses were the "sweetest." She had glued little heart-shaped candies with little messages like "You're the greatest" and "I luv u" all around hers.

"I have glasses, too," announced Amber, as she pulled hers from her pocket.

"Would you like some decorations?" asked Colleen, handing her two little silk butterflies with some sticky putty that wouldn't damage her glasses.

What a sight they all were! They had such a good time sharing tea and treats. As they sipped their tea, Colleen began. "My mother told me about games young ladies can play and still be polite and ladylike at parties. They are called 'parlor games' because you can play them sitting in the parlor."

"Do you know one?" asked Amber.

"I do," continued Colleen. "It is called Silly Aunt Tilly. This is how it's played. Aunt Tilly only likes certain things and Aunt Tilly dislikes other things. Aunt Tilly has a reason for liking certain things, and you have to figure it out by guessing something she likes and something she doesn't like. I will start by giving you a clue and will let you know if your answer is

LOVE IS THE VERY BEST

right or wrong, okay? Silly Aunt Tilly likes tea, but she doesn't like coffee."

"That's easy!" Maggie declared. "Silly Aunt Tilly likes sugar, but she doesn't like cream."

"No," said Colleen mysteriously, "that's not right."

"Well," said Amber with a sly smile, "does she ride trains but not airplanes?"

"As a matter of fact, she does," replied Colleen.

"Silly Aunt Tilly likes cats but she doesn't like dogs," tried Caroline.

"I'm afraid not."

"Does she like a piano but not a violin?" asked Maggie.

"No, again."

"But at a concert in the park, she prefers a trombone to a saxophone," said Amber with confidence.

Maggie and Caroline were really puzzled.

"I'll give you one more clue," offered Colleen. "Silly Aunt Tilly likes Tuesday but not Wednesday."

"We give up!" Maggie and Caroline threw up their hands.

"Would you like to tell them, Amber?" asked Colleen.

"Silly Aunt Tilly only likes things that begin with the letter 'T'!"

"Parlor games are fun," decided Maggie, "they *tickle* the brain!"

"I agree with Aunt Tilly," said Amber. "I like all things *tea*, especially tea parties with friends!"

I praise you because you made me in
an amazing and wonderful way.
What you have done is wonderful.

Psalm 139:14

Big Sisters
Are Special
A Garden of Hope Tea

I saw a big pink bow on the mailbox at Sarah's house today," Colleen reported to Maggie as she helped her weed her flowers.

"You mean the new baby is here?" Colleen asked excitedly, almost spilling her watering can.

"Yes, it's a little girl, and Sarah is a big sister now!"

"Wow! I bet she feels important."

"I'm not so sure," Maggie doubted. "I think all the excitement over the baby is making her feel a little left out."

"It sounds like she needs to know that big sisters are as important as babies," piped up Rosebeary.

"Do you think we could give her hope that she will be a special big sister?" Colleen wondered.

"H-m-m-m," Maggie thought out loud, "I don't know how."

"Well," said Upsi-Daisy, "I've noticed how tenderly you care for the little flowers in your garden."

"Yes," said Rosebeary, with another hint,

"it's almost like they have a big sister!"

"I do love these little flowers," admitted Colleen, "and they're not even people—they are just plants. What an important thing it is to care for little people."

"Seeing how you care for your garden might give her hope that she can be important to her baby sister," Bunnita pointed out.

"You know," Maggie looked around, "this garden would be a pretty place for a tea party!"

Bunnita's ears perked up. "What a lovely idea! Tea in the garden. Can we have carrot cake?"

"Yes!" laughed Colleen. "And we'll use the garden to share faith, hope, and love with Sarah!"

Maggie and Colleen gathered Caroline

TEATIME CRAFT
Wheelbarrow Planters

You will need…

- *potting soil*
- *plastic detergent scoop (have your mom start saving these for you)*
- *caps from plastic milk containers (you will need 2 per planter)*
- *plant or flower seed of choice*

Glue a cap on each side of the plastic scoop for "wheels." When these are dry, fill the scoop with potting soil and the plant or seed you have chosen.

and Amber for a lunchtime tea for Sarah. With the birds singing and butterflies flitting and fluttering about, it was delightful! There were no babies at this tea party—only encouragement for a girl with new opportunities. After all the sandwiches, treats, and tea were gone, Caroline asked Sarah, "How do you like having a baby sister?"

"Well…" started Sarah, "she's really tiny and cute but she needs my mother and father more than she needs me. She's not big enough to play with."

Colleen had thought a lot about how caring for a little sister could be like caring for a garden. She had planned a unique party favor. She cleared away the cups and saucers and plates and placed a plastic scoop from a laundry detergent box in front of each girl, along with two caps from milk jugs.

"What is this?" they all wondered.

"We're going to plant a little flower in a garden wheelbarrow." She showed them how to place the scoop with the handle up and glue a "wheel" (bottlecap) on each side of the scoop. She then gave each girl a small impatiens plant and a spoon to scoop potting soil from a bowl on the table.

While they planted, Colleen began to point out all the things Sarah could do for her little sister to help her thrive like the little flowers. "If you 'water' your little sister with kind words and love, her heart will be as beautiful as these little flowers."

"And encouragement is the best dirt for her little roots. You can teach her all the things you know—from tying her shoes to riding a bicycle. And help her do a good job," Maggie added.

"There are things that could harm your little sister—like bugs!" cautioned Caroline. "You can help your parents watch out for them and keep her safe."

"And you can share faith with her as she grows," encouraged Rosebeary.

"And the hope of spring," added Bunnita.

"And always love her," smiled Upsi-Daisy. "She needs your love."

Sarah looked at the little flower and thought about her baby sister. "She needs me!" she exclaimed. "And Mother and Daddy need me to share with her what they're teaching me. I've been given a very important job. I got a big gift when I got a baby sister, didn't I?"

"Oh, yes, and she got a wonderful gift too— a sweet big sister," agreed Colleen, "who can teach her about tea parties!"

TEATIME TREAT
Sweet Sandwiches

Break apart graham crackers into squares (the cinnamon-sugar graham crackers are great!). Spread on ready-made frosting and make into little sandwiches. These sweet treats are sure to be a teatime favorite.

Love is patient and kind.

1 CORINTHIANS 13:4

He's Got the Whole World In His Hands

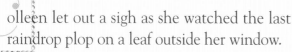

Faith in the Storm Tea

Colleen let out a sigh as she watched the last raindrop plop on a leaf outside her window.

"I thought we were having tea this afternoon," said Bunnita hopefully.

"Everyone else is busy except for Caroline. And she won't come if it's raining," explained Colleen.

"But the rain just stopped," said Rosebeary, sticking her paw out the window.

"I know, but it's beginning to cloud up again," said Colleen.

"Why won't she come?" wondered Bunnita and Rosebeary.

"She's afraid of thunder and lightning and the noise of rain. She is afraid to leave her house."

"Maybe we could encourage her to have faith and make that fear go away!" suggested Rosebeary.

"But how?" asked Colleen.

"I have an idea." Bunnita's ears perked up. "Let's take your doll furniture and dolls and arrange them carefully in the center of the table and set the table for tea."

"And then," Rosebeary added, "we'll take our brightest umbrellas and walk over to her house and bring her back with us before another storm starts."

"But how will the doll furniture show her that she's safe?" puzzled Colleen.

"Well," said Bunnita, "think about how carefully you move and place your furniture

and how carefully you watch over your dolls."

"Oh! I see!" exclaimed Colleen, as she ran for her umbrella.

Caroline couldn't resist venturing out for a tea party when she saw their bright umbrellas and hopeful faces. As they all pulled up chairs around Colleen's table for a cozy little tea, the sun went behind the clouds and they heard the distant rumble of thunder.

"I have to go home," Caroline said, pushing her chair back from the table. "We might have a storm."

"No, wait," said Colleen. "Do you see my doll furniture and my dolls on the table?"

"Yes, but what do they have to do with a storm?" asked Caroline.

"Well, I don't always have them on the table. Sometimes they're in my dollhouse or on a shelf. But I always take very good care of them no matter where I place them. And I watch out for them. Our heavenly Father, who created us, loves us very much and wants the best for us too! He watches over you and me day and night, rain or shine! He knows that you're at my house and will take good care of you here or wherever you are."

"He loves you even more than Colleen loves her dolls," added Upsi-Daisy.

"You're right," agreed Caroline thoughtfully. "God will take care of me just as well here as at home. I don't need to be afraid. He knows exactly where I am!"

Colleen poured the warm tea, and they passed yummy treats around the table. The rhythm of the rain with the tinkling of the wind chime outside began to sound like music to Caroline.

When the rain had stopped, they started to walk Caroline home and then stopped. It didn't take them long to pull off their socks and shoes. They splashed barefooted in the puddles all the way to Caroline's house.

"I'm thankful for the rain," she giggled. "It brings fun!" 🌸

I have taken care of you
from your birth…
I made you and will take care of you.
ISAIAH 46:3-4

Just
For Mom
Pretty as a Picture Tea

Colleen closed the back door behind her as she walked into her mother's cheery yellow kitchen.

"You look tired," her mother observed as she poured a glass of milk and got some oatmeal cookies for her. "Where have you been?"

"Looking," said Colleen, "just looking."

"Have you lost something?"

"No, ma'am," said Colleen, as she thanked her mother for the refreshments and climbed the stairs to her room.

"I hope," Colleen said to Bunnita, Rosebeary, and Upsi-Daisy, "that you all have some ideas because I don't. I've looked *everywhere* for somebody in need of faith, hope, or love, and I can't find anyone to have a tea party for! Everybody I found is doing great! In fact, everybody is so happy that it's almost discouraging. Nobody needs a tea party!"

"Oh, everyone needs a tea party," Rosebeary assured her.

"And you don't have to find someone who is sad or lonely to show love," encouraged Upsi-Daisy. "Nobody ever has too much love!"

Colleen looked at the cookies in her hand. Her mother was always sharing love. Who could deserve a tea party more than her mother?

"You're right," Colleen said aloud, "a tea party would be a wonderful way to show love to my mother—a mother-daughter tea party! I could ask Sarah, Maggie, Caroline, and Amber to come with their mothers, too."

"And we could have carrot cake again," Bunnita said, both pleased and hopeful at her menu suggestion.

"Uh-oh!" Colleen suddenly realized that she had never prepared a tea party for grownups.

Just then Gramma Claire popped her head in the door. "I hear some happy chatter in here. Are you tea party partners cooking something up?"

"We are!" answered Colleen emphatically. "And you're just the person we need."

Colleen knew Gramma Claire would keep their plans a secret and help them. Since Gramma Claire had come to live in their house, Colleen had found out that her grandmother knew how to do some pretty neat things.

The next day, as soon as Colleen's mother left for the market, Maggie, Caroline, Amber, and Sarah all gathered around the kitchen table at Colleen's house. Each had brought her own stash of buttons from her mother's button jar.

As they leaned their elbows on the table in anticipation, all eyes were on Gramma Claire as she showed them a finished example of the picture frame they were going to make.

"Oh, my mother will love it," Maggie exclaimed.

"Mine, too!" they all agreed.

Gramma Claire had already mixed up clay for them made of salt water and cornstarch.

The girls shared rolling pins as they each rolled out the clay, dusting it with cornstarch. Amber cut out her frame first, cutting out a large heart with a heart-shaped cookie cutter and then cutting out the center with a smaller cookie cutter. Carefully, she lifted the frame and placed it on a cookie sheet dusted with

TEATIME CRAFT
Cookie Cutter Clay

2 cups salt
2/3 cup water
1 cup cornstarch
1/2 cup cold water

Be sure to ask an adult to help you. Mix salt with water in saucepan. Stir and boil. Add cornstarch and cold water. Heat until mixture gets thick. Roll out dough on board floured with cornstarch. Cut shapes out with a cookie cutter, then let dry. When thoroughly dry, paint or decorate.

cornstarch. Soon, six neat frames were lined up in a row—six because Colleen made one for Gramma Claire, too.

"Well, let's see. What could we do while these frames dry?" Gramma Claire asked, playfully holding up the cookie cutters.

"Let's make cookies!" Maggie suggested.

"And eat cookies!" Caroline added.

"Not just cookies," said Gramma Claire, "snickerdoodles."

Just the name made them all giggle in delight. Gramma Claire's orange spice tea was absolutely yummy with the warm cookies they pulled from the oven. While they munched, they planned the other details of the party. They had enough snickerdoodles left to store tightly in a tin for the party.

When the frames were dry enough, the girls embellished them by gluing on buttons to make a heart surrounded by memories. Then they left them with Gramma Claire for safekeeping.

The mothers and daughters arrived on Saturday afternoon to find the tea table covered with an heirloom quilt and topped by a square lace tablecloth. At each mother's place was a photo of her as a little girl. By the time everyone had matched each mother with her own childhood photo, they were all chatting like old friends, recalling their pigtails, freckles, and their favorite childhood memories.

The girls truly honored their mothers by behaving like perfect little ladies. Gramma Claire insisted on serving so that the girls could all sit with their mothers.

Her face just beamed as she saw in these girls the reflection of the loveliness of their mothers.

As each mother and daughter arrived, Gramma Claire had taken an instant photo of them together. While the mothers and daughters enjoyed their last cup of tea, she quickly put each photo into the frame that was made for it. One by one the girls presented their mothers with the photo and frame they had made for them. All the mothers were so thankful for such a thoughtful gift and

the memory of such a special party.

"Isn't it wonderful to see how each generation helps complete the pretty picture of love!" said Maggie's mother, comparing her childhood photo to the new one of her and Maggie.

"I hope that one day when I am a mother, I find this photo of my mother and me beside my plate at a tea party," said Colleen wistfully, never wanting tea parties to end.

"Someday, you will be somebody's mother," said Colleen's mother with a hug, "but you will always be my daughter, and we shall always have tea parties. Isn't that right, Mother?" As she turned to Gramma Claire, Caroline's mother quickly snapped a photo of the three of them together.

"We have a tea party tradition!" Gramma Claire said with a big smile.

If we love each other, God lives in us.
If we love each other, God's love has
reached its goal.

1 JOHN 4:12

TEATIME TREAT
Snickerdoodle Cookies

1 1/4 cup margarine (do not use butter)
2 cups granulated sugar
2 3/4 cups all-purpose flour
1 teaspoon baking powder
1/2 teaspoon salt
2 eggs
2 teaspoons vanilla extract
1/3 cup sour cream
1/3 cup granulated sugar
1/3 cup cinnamon

Ask an adult to help you with this recipe. Preheat oven to 350 degrees. In medium bowl, combine flour, baking powder, and salt; set aside. In a small bowl or saucer, combine 1/3 cup sugar and 1/3 cup cinnamon; set aside. In a large bowl, cream together margarine and 2 cups sugar until fluffy. Beat in the eggs one at a time. Add vanilla. Stir in the dry ingredients in the medium bowl just until blended. The dough will be very soft, so you may want to refrigerate the dough until it is firm (this makes it easier to handle). Roll the dough into walnut-sized balls, and roll half of the ball in the sugar/cinnamon mixture. Place cookies on an ungreased baking sheet sugar side up. Bake for 8 to 10 minutes in preheated oven, until lightly brown at the edges. Cool cookies on the baking sheet for 3 to 5 minutes before removing to a wire rack for further cooling. (The purpose for this is that the cookies are very soft, and they need to firm a bit before being removed from the baking sheet.)

This recipe will make 60 to 75 cookies, depending on the size you roll the cookie balls.

Where Is Joy?

Serving a Cup of Joy Tea

Miss Sandy smiled as she watched Colleen pulling her wagon down the sidewalk to her tearoom. They were a sight! Rosebeary was holding on tightly as they bounced along with the wind blowing through Bunnita's ears and ruffling Upsi-Daisy's petals. Colleen was indeed in a hurry!

"We're here for my tea party!" Colleen announced at the front porch, pausing to catch her breath.

"I've been looking forward to this," Miss Sandy said smiling. "I want to hear all about your tea parties. Did you have fun? Would you like to have more tea parties?"

"Oh, Miss Sandy," Colleen replied with enthusiasm, "there is no end to the way we can show faith, hope, and love with tea parties. We're just getting started!"

TEATIME TREAT
Pineapple Cream Cheese Sandwiches

Drain one 15-ounce can of crushed pineapple very well. Mix the pineapple into 8 ounces of softened cream cheese. Next, spread this mixture on your favorite bread and top with a bread slice. For decorative fun, use a cookie cutter to cut the sandwich into a fun shape.

Bunnita, Rosebeary, and Upsi-Daisy hopped up on their chairs at the tea table. Colleen looked for an extra chair. She was expecting someone new to teach her about "joy." But there was no extra chair. When Miss Sandy turned to pour Rosebeary some tea, Colleen even lifted the tablecloth and peeked under the table.

Miss Sandy calmly continued to pour the strawberry tea and serve pineapple-cream cheese sandwiches, pound cake hearts, and apple slices. She was in no hurry to explain the "joy" teacup to Colleen. She wanted to hear every detail of every party.

"Colleen helped Caroline have the faith to not be afraid," Rosebeary announced proudly.

"She served her friends with love," approved Upsi-Daisy, "and they were sweet to each other."

"We had carrot cake twice," Bunnita added with a smile.

"Ahem," Rosebeary cleared her throat.

"Oh," Bunnita added sheepishly, "and

Colleen did a lovely job of giving her friends hope when they needed it."

"Please, Miss Sandy," pleaded Colleen, "I can't stand the suspense. Rosebeary has so patiently pointed out the need for faith to me, Bunnita has helped me see when a friend needs hope, and Upsi-Daisy has taught me that love is the very best. But who is going to help me share joy?"

TEATIME TREAT
Pound Cake Hearts

Cut your pound cake (store-bought or homemade) into 1/2-inch-thick slices. Next, cut the slices into heart shapes with a cookie cutter. Then "frost" each heart with strawberry jam to create tasty, cheery red hearts for dessert.

"Why, you are Colleen," said Miss Sandy with a smile.

"Me?"

"Yes. All of your birthday gifts were designed to help you see that your life is a gift. Since the moment you were born, you have been a special gift to your family and everyone around you. You bring joy to others just by being you. But you bring joy to yourself by serving others. And, as you have learned, there's no better way to do that than by sharing faith, hope, and love."

"Thank you, Miss Sandy, for all my gifts. You know, serving others and making others happy has brought *me* so much joy," Colleen realized. "The joy cup will always be my favorite!"

TEATIME TREAT
Anywhere You Go Cookies

Spread creamy peanut butter between two vanilla wafers for a homemade travel-anywhere-cookie-sandwich treat.

Be full of joy in the Lord always.
I will say it again, be full of joy.

PHILIPPIANS 4:4

Dear Young Friend,

Just like Colleen, you are a gift and a joy to those who know and love you. Have you been thinking about ways that you can share faith, hope, and love? Are you planning a tea party?

I invite you to share the joy!

Miss Sandy